Contents

The Magic Castle   page 3
A poem about a wizard and wishes
Clare Bevan

The Wizard's Wish Magnet   page 23
Louise Glasspoole

CAMBRIDGE UNIVERSITY PRESS

CAMBRIDGE UNIVERSITY PRESS
Cambridge, New York, Melbourne, Madrid, Cape Town, Singapore, São Paulo

Cambridge University Press
The Edinburgh Building, Cambridge CB2 8RU, UK

www.cambridge.org
Information on this title: www.cambridge.org/9780521704823

© Cambridge University Press 2007

This publication is in copyright. Subject to statutory exception
and to the provisions of relevant collective licensing agreements,
no reproduction of any part may take place without the written
permission of Cambridge University Press.

First published 2007

Printed in the United Kingdom at the University Press, Cambridge

A catalogue record for this publication is available from the British Library

ISBN 978-0-521-70482-3 paperback

ACKNOWLEDGEMENTS

Cover
Frances Castle

Artwork
The Magic Castle: Frances Castle
The Wizard's Wish Magnet: Frances Castle

Texts
'The Magic Castle' by Clare Bevan
'The Wizard's Wish Magnet' by Louise Glasspoole

Layout and typesetting by eMC Design Ltd, www.emcdesign.org.uk

The Magic Castle

A poem about a wizard and wishes
by Clare Bevan

4

The Magic Castle

Imagine a misty castle,
Imagine a twisty stair,
Climb to the top of the Wizard's tower ...
He makes his magic there!

Tiptoe away to the playroom,
Creep as a spider creeps,
Look for the glittery doll's house where
A fairy princess sleeps.

Scamper along to the kitchen.
Careful! The floorboard creaks.
A mouse prince hides in the biscuit tin
And sadly, sadly squeaks.

Down again, down to the dungeon
As dark as a midnight sky.
Deep in the shadows a dragon wakes
So jump on her tail – and fly!

The Wise Wizard

At the top of a dizzy and dangerous stair,
In a cobwebby room, on a cobwebby chair,
You will find the Wise Wizard, with stars in his hair.

His feathery robe seems to flutter like wings,
His thumbs and his fingers wear magical rings,
From his hat (which is purple) a pet spider swings.

With his willowy wand, with a swirl and a swish,
He can talk to a dragon, a mouse or a fish.
He can cast any spell. He can grant any wish.

The Fairy Princess

The Fairy Princess
In her ivy-green dress —
She lives in the doll's house, alone.
No beetle, no bee,
No bugs come to see
The birthday balloons round her throne.

The Fairy Princess,
In her river-blue dress –
She dreams of a friend who will share
The tiny, iced cakes,
She mixes and bakes
For her birthday ... but no-one is there.

The Fairy Princess
In her winter-white dress –
She wishes for somebody small.
A brave, royal mouse
Who will visit her house
And dance at her Grand
   Birthday Ball.

The Kitchen Mouse Rap

The Kitchen Mouse –
He is forced to float
Around the sink
In a gravy boat.

He rubs and scrubs
At the castle plates
With a holly leaf –
It's a job he HATES.
There are spoons to scrape,
There are jugs to rinse,
As he sadly squeaks:
"I was once a prince …

But I lost my crown
And my treasure box
With its crafty key
And its clever locks.
If I make a wish,
If I find them all,
Perhaps I'll dance
At the Birthday Ball."

So he scurries back
To his biscuit tin
Where he sadly squeaks:
"I am growing thin,
But I once ate cakes
From a golden dish."
Then he eats his crumbs ...
And he makes his wish.

The Dungeon Dragon

Beware of the Dragon! She's massive and mean. She's scary and scaly. She's ghastly and green.

Don't wobble her wings. Don't creep near her claws. She'll suddenly open her horrible jaws.

She'll fry you with flames. She'll turn you to toast.
She'll breathe on your boots till they sizzle and roast.

Only the Wizard, so wise and so old,
Can make her feel shivery, quivery cold.

The Kitchen Mouse speaks. (He is under a spell.)
The Dragon just winks! (She's been magicked as well.)

She twitches her tail and she opens a box —
It has one crafty key. It has two clever locks.

She offers the Mouse Prince his own royal crown.
A big bag of gold and a small velvet gown.

Then she flies him away to the Fairy Princess,
Who dances for joy in her new birthday dress.

Clare Bevan

Questions

Discuss these questions with the child/children as you read the book together.

- Why do you think the Mouse Prince might be hiding in the biscuit tin? (page 7)
- Who lives in the dungeon? (page 8)
- Why are there balloons round the Fairy Princess's throne? Who do you think put them there? (page 11)
- How do you think she is feeling? Why? (page 12)
- What does the mouse use the holly leaf for? (page 15)
- What do you think might have happened to his crown and treasure box? (page 16)
- What is he going to wish for? (page 16)
- Whose Birthday Ball is it? (page 16)
- Why do you think the mouse is growing thin? (page 17)
- Is the dragon frightening? Which words or phrases show this? (page 18)
- Do you think the Wizard is afraid of the dragon? What makes you think this? (page 19)
- What do you think happened to the mouse's crown and treasure box? (page 21)
- Is there a happy ending for the Fairy Princess and the Mouse Prince? (page 21)

The Wizard's Wish Magnet

Louise Glasspoole

A wizard in his magic tower tells the world about his power.

This month's interview in *Wizarding World* magazine is with Wilberforce the Wise. Wilberforce, please tell our readers more about the magic that you do.

Just lately I've been up here here in my tower, doing some useful magic. Last week, I bought this fantastic new machine. It's called a Wish Magnet, and I finished setting it up yesterday. The machine pulls all wishes inside it. This morning, the machine pulled in some wishes from inside this castle. One was from a fairy princess, and the other came from a mouse who used to be a prince. Later this week, I will think about whether I should grant their wishes.

Thank you, Wilberforce. I will come to interview you again soon. Our readers would love to hear about all the different wishes that the Wish Magnet has pulled in.

Her party takes place on Saturday night, but the Princess doesn't know who to invite.

You are invited to
My Grand Birthday Ball
Lots of dancing and all the cake you can eat.

Saturday 13th June, 8pm

Reply to: The Doll's House
　　　　　The Play Room
　　　　　Wizard's Castle
　　　　　1, The Hill
　　　　　Villageton

Lady Mermaid
Craggy Rocks

Townley-on-Sea

Dear Lady Mermaid,

I hope you are well and that you haven't been caught up in any nets. I have sent you an invitation to my **Birthday Ball**, which is on Saturday. I expect you won't be able to come, because my doll's house is so far from the sea where you live.

I have sent lots of invitations, but I don't know if anybody will be able to come. I really wish a handsome mouse prince would come. But I don't suppose he will. I will have to eat all the cakes myself.

If you do come, please bring as many friends as you can!

Best wishes,

Titania

HRH Princess Titania of the Doll's House

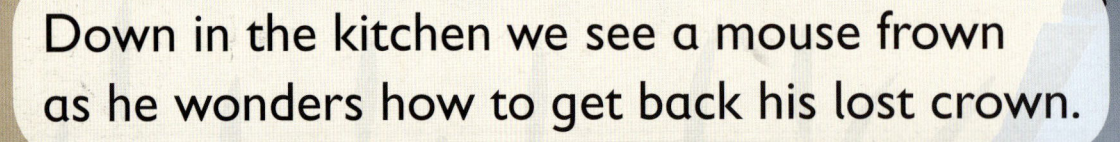

Down in the kitchen we see a mouse frown as he wonders how to get back his lost crown.

LOST

Small, shiny crown. Sturdy chest with several key holes. Possibly dropped by a passing dragon

If found please bring to
Mr A Mouse
Castle Kitchen,
Wizard's Castle
1 The Hill
Villageton

Thursday 11th June

There was a lovely smell of baking in the air today. It reminded me of the cakes that the Fairy Princess baked, and that I used to eat from my golden dish.

On Saturday, it will be the Fairy Princess's birthday.

This time last year, I was getting ready for her Birthday Ball. I am so sad that I can't go this year. I was very silly to give my crown and treasure box to that dragon. I thought she would give them back, but she took them away to her den.

So now I have lost them.

I've been wishing that they would come back to me. Yesterday, I even left some notes around the village.

I don't have a crown, so the other mice think I am only pretending to be a prince. They gave me this job doing the washing up as a punishment. It is the worst job in all Mouseketania.

Perhaps if I make more wishes, I'll get my crown and treasure box back. I could make a wish for each dish I wash tonight. That might do it!

35

Back in the tower, going through his list, the Wizard checks to see nothing's been missed.

WISHES RECEIVED

Wish 1
The Fairy Princess wants a prince to come to her birthday ball.

Wish 2 -
The mouse that is working in the kitchen used to be a prince! He wants his crown and treasure box back. He thinks that the Dragon has them.

ONE MONTH LATER

The Princess danced with her prince after all. Soon they'll be planning their wedding ball.

Her Royal Highness Princess Titania of the Doll's House has announced her engagement to Prince Arthur of Mouseketania. Princess, please tell us about why you decided to get married.

It all happened at my birthday ball. I had been getting ready for it all week. I baked lots of cakes and chose a dress, but I didn't know if anyone would come. I wished that the Mouse Prince would come, like he did last year. I didn't think that my wish could come true. But on the night of the ball, Arthur arrived on the back of a large, green dragon!

Questions

Discuss these questions with the child/children as you read the book together.

- Where have you seen the Wizard before? (page 24)
- What do you think the Fairy Princess wished for? (page 25)
- What did the Mouse Prince wish for? (page 25)
- What words are used on the notice to describe the crown? (page 28)
- What word is used to describe the chest? (page 28)
- Who do you think has written this diary? (page 29)
- What date was the Mouse Prince's diary written? (page 29)
- When is the Princess's birthday? (page 30)
- Why do the other mice think he is only pretending to be a prince? (page 32)
- What job does he have to do? (page 32)
- Does he like his job? How do you know? (page 32)
- Will there be a happy ending? Why do you think this? (page 34)
- Do you think the Wizard will grant their wishes? (page 34)